This Book Belongs to:

Ms. Rabia

Hugs & Kisses from Suzie Belle ♥
(Paula Cater)
2016

All rights reserved. No part of this book shall be reproduced or transmitted in any form or by any means, electronic, mechanical, magnetic, photographic including photocopying, recording or by any information storage and retrieval system, without prior written permission of the publisher. No patent liability is assumed with respect to the use of the information contained herein. Although every precaution has been taken in the preparation of this book, the publisher and author assume no responsibility for errors or omissions. Neither is any liability assumed for damages resulting from the use of the information contained herein.

Copyright © 2016 by Ann Averitt & Paula Caten

ISBN 978-1-4958-1037-4 Paperback
ISBN 978-1-4958-1002-2 eBook

This is a work of fiction. Names, characters, places, and incidents either are the product of the author's imagination or are used fictitiously. Any resemblance to actual events or locales or persons, living or dead, is entirely coincidental.

Printed in the United States of America

Published April 2016

INFINITY PUBLISHING
1094 New DeHaven Street, Suite 100
West Conshohocken, PA 19428-2713
Toll-free (877) BUY BOOK
Local Phone (610) 941-9999
Fax (610) 941-9959
Info@buybooksontheweb.com
www.buybooksontheweb.com

Suzie Belle
and the Dress Dilemma

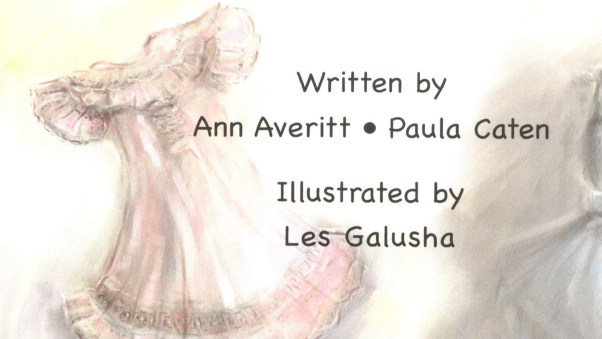

Written by
Ann Averitt • Paula Caten

Illustrated by
Les Galusha

There was excitement in Suzie Belle's closet.

Satin, Lace, Plaid, Torn, and Brown were anxiously waiting for the day to begin.
They knew it was Monday, and Suzie Belle would be going to school.

"Which one of us will Suzie Belle wear today?" they asked themselves. Each dress burst with anticipation, hoping to be the lucky one chosen.

Suzie Belle threw open the closet door.
She was wearing her fuzzy slippers, and her hair was all atangle, but her eyes were bright as she greeted her friends, the dresses.

"Good morning, Dresses," she chirped.
"Guess what day this is."

"Monday, Monday!"
the dresses chorused.

"It's a school day.
Who wants to go to school with me?"
Suzie Belle asked.

Suzie Belle examined the dresses carefully. Which one should she choose? She reached for the beautiful dress made of shiny satin.

"No, too fancy!"

As she continued down the row of dresses, a tear slipped out of Satin's eye.

"If only I were not so elegant!" Satin thought.

Suzie Belle kept looking.

"Maybe the pink lacy one. No, I must save that one for something special too."

"Awwww!"
moaned Lace.

"How about the red and blue plaid?
No, I wore that two times last week."

"That's not fair!"

Plaid said with a scowl.

"Maybe this pretty green one?
No, it has a tear that Mother forgot to fix."

Finally Suzie Belle's eyes landed on her old friend, the plain brown dress.

It was not torn. It was not plaid, lace or satin.

It was the perfect dress for Suzie Belle because it was soft and comfy from having been worn and washed so many times. It fit just right, and it never showed playground dirt or lunchroom stains.

Suzie Belle loved it!

Suzie Belle slipped on her old friend Brown and happily left for school. Brown smiled and waved at the other dresses as she flitted out the door.

All day the forsaken dresses hung in the dark, quiet closet waiting for Suzie Belle and Brown to come home. The dresses were sad and lonely, but they did not give up. During that long, boring Monday, each little dress was thinking,

"I wonder what Brown and Suzie Belle are doing at school today?"

"Are they painting pretty pictures?"

"Are they playing hopscotch or tag?"

"Maybe I will go to school tomorrow."

At last the closet door opened. Suzie Belle was finally home from school.

The dresses wanted to know about Brown's day at school. Brown was tired, but she willingly told them all about her adventures.

"It was wonderful!"
she said proudly.

"In the morning we read a mystery story, and in the afternoon we worked addition problems on the blackboard."

"Lunch was peanut butter and jelly sandwiches with yummy chocolate cake for dessert. At recess we played jacks and jump rope. On our bus ride home, we sat with Suzie Belle's best friend Betsy."

"Wow!" exclaimed the dresses.

"We love school!"

The rest of the week sped by quickly. Suzie Belle was a kind little girl, so she tried to be fair to each of her dresses.

Plaid went to school on Tuesday.

Torn made a trip to the sewing machine with Mother and was ready for school on Wednesday.

On Thursday there was a dress-up mother-daughter tea after school. All the girls were told to wear their finest clothes. Suzie Belle went to the closet and pulled out her two most beautiful dresses, Satin and Lace.

She danced around the room with them, trying to decide which one would be perfect for the tea. It was so hard to decide.

As she was dancing with Lace, Suzie Belle heard Mother calling, "It's time to go. We don't want to be late!" Suzie Belle quickly pulled Lace over her head, tossed Satin on a nearby chair, and hurried out the door with Mother.

Lace was thrilled...

...but Satin was broken hearted again.

On Friday morning Suzie Belle was tired and sleepy. She had studied hard all week and had been to an activity every day after school. With her eyes half closed, she reached into her closet and pulled out her old friend Brown.

"Sorry, Girls!" she sighed.

She closed the door, shutting out the disappointed sounds escaping from the other dresses.

On Saturday morning as Suzie Belle was cleaning her room, she noticed that Satin was still draped over the chair, looking sad and dejected.

"Oh, you poor thing! I forgot to hang you up, and you didn't even get to go anywhere this week!

Would you like to have a tea party?"

Satin wasn't sure what a tea party was, but it sounded interesting. "Maybe," she said as she wiped away her tears and tried to smile.

19

Suzie Belle finished cleaning her room in a flash and spent the rest of the morning preparing for Satin's tea party.

She set up a little table and created four places: one for herself, one for her favorite doll, another for Teddy Bear, and one for her little dog Max.

She went outside and picked a bouquet of flowers for the center of the table. She rummaged through her mother's sewing basket until she found the perfect ribbon to tie on each chair.

She searched her toy box and brought out her tea set. When everything was ready, she ran excitedly to get her mother.

"Look at my tea party!" she exclaimed.

"Oh, it's beautiful!" said Mother. "What will you serve?"

"Oh, no! I didn't think of that," Suzie Belle cried. "What will I do?"

"Don't worry," her mother reassured her. "I'll find you some juice and cookies while you get dressed for the party."

"Oh, thanks!" said Suzie Belle as she turned to Satin. "Are you ready?" she asked. Satin glowed. So Suzie Belle carefully pulled Satin over her head, looked in the mirror, and asked, "How do we look?"

"We look BEAUTIFUL!" sighed Satin.

When Satin saw everything that Suzie Belle had done -- the place mats, the flowers, the ribbons, -- she could hardly believe her eyes.

"For me?" she gasped.

"I'm the happiest dress in the closet!"

To Cameron Averitt Bobbitt

(2000-2006)

Who loved princess dresses and tea parties

CPSIA information can be obtained at www.ICGtesting.com
Printed in the USA
LVIW01n0120310516
490372LV00004B/11